Aaron L. Lindsley

Farewell sermon of Rev. A. L. Lindsley, D.D.

delivered upon closing his ministry in the First Presbyterian Church,

Portland, Oregon

Aaron L. Lindsley

Farewell sermon of Rev. A. L. Lindsley, D.D.
delivered upon closing his ministry in the First Presbyterian Church, Portland, Oregon

ISBN/EAN: 9783337266646

Printed in Europe, USA, Canada, Australia, Japan

Cover: Foto ©Lupo / pixelio.de

More available books at **www.hansebooks.com**

FAREWELL SERMON

OF

REV. A. L. LINDSLEY, D. D.,

DELIVERED UPON CLOSING HIS
MINISTRY IN THE

First Presbyterian Church,

PORTLAND, OREGON.

Together with his Letter of Resignation, the Action of the Presbytery,
and of the Congregation, and the Address
of the Rev. E. W. Garner, D. D., in declaring the pulpit vacant.

———————————

PORTLAND, OREGON.
1886.

Grace be unto you, and peace, from God our Father and from the Lord Jesus Christ. I thank my God always on your behalf, for the grace of God which is given you by Jesus Christ: that in every thing ye are enriched by him, in all utterance, and in all knowledge; even as the testimony of Christ was confirmed in you: so that ye come behind in no gift; waiting for the coming of our Lord Jesus Christ: who shall also confirm you unto the end, that ye may be blameless in the day of our Lord Jesus Christ.—*I. Cor. 1:3-8.*

Dr. Lindsley's Letter of Resignation.

To the First Presbyterian Church
and Congregation, of Portland:

DEAR BRETHREN AND FRIENDS:—With the assent of the Session I respectfully ask you to unite with me in a request to Presbytery to dissolve the pastoral relation existing between us.

I desire this release in order to devote myself to the professorship to which I have been appointed in our Theological Seminary.

There are solemn and responsible ties existing between a pastor and the people of his charge, and the relationship should not be dissolved for any consideration which will not bear the approbation of an enlightened conscience. If I were to yield to the dictates of my heart, I should not make this petition. The growing years have made my official relations to you more and more comprehensive, and my affection for you more tender and abiding. The official relation may cease, but my love and friendship for you, death cannot terminate.

I have viewed this subject in every light, and having earnestly sought the guidance of God's spirit, it appears to me that He calls me to this new occupation. I have been lead to regard it as the most important appointment that any man could receive. There is no higher calling than the pastoral relation, and the training of those who occupy it, must be the highest responsibility that can ever fall upon any man.

It is proper for me to say that I did not seek this appointment. When first addressed upon the subject, I could only say that I would give it serious consideration.

There are peculiarities connected with my election to this position that are quite remarkable and almost deprive me of my liberty of choice.

1. My nomination was made by the concurrence of our whole Synod. A similar degree of unanimity, it is believed, exists in the other Synod on this coast, the Synod of the Pacific. I have received expressions of

confidence and congratulations from all parts of the Church, and many friends outside of it.

2. The brethren concerned in the Seminary think that my acceptance will give a new impulse to Ministerial education on this coast, and help to establish our Seminary upon a firm basis and make it popular among the churches. From every direction I have heard the voices of Christian people who think it is my duty to accept the appointment.

The indications of God's will which come to me from my brethren, find a response in my own mind. The school is yet in its infancy, and much remains to be done to equip it and make it adequate to the demands of the present time, for the furtherance of the gospel. In this department of the Seminary work I should expect to engage.

Many of you have said that there is evidently the guiding hand of God in it, as well as personal fitness for the work, and these two circumstances combine to gain their consent to sever the pastoral tie, while they also serve to encourage your pastor ; for no human judgment can have so much weight in settling and satisfying my own mind, as the deliberate conclusions of the intelligent and discriminating people to whom I have ministered, and who have so often encouraged me by their devout attention and their appreciation of my pastoral labors.

Notice was given on Thursday evening, and in the daily papers, of my intention to offer my resignation of the pastoral office, and this action has been expected for some time past. Although I propose not to leave you for a few weeks, it will serve the convenience of the Presbytery if you will take action to-day, in order that the whole subject may be laid before that body at its next regular meeting. The day for declaring the pulpit vacant, can be chosen after consultation at Presbytery.

To the guidance of the Church's Head, and to your decision, I commit this request, and subscribe myself,

The shepherd of the flock under Christ, and your servant, for His sake, who gave His life for the sheep,

A. L. LINDSLEY.

PORTLAND, OR., Oct. 10th, 1886.

Action of the Presbytery.

WHEREAS, Rev. A. L. Lindsley, D. D., has done a most faithful and praiseworthy work during his pastorate of eighteen years, finding the church with less than one hundred members, burdened with a heavy indebtedness, and under his faithful direction has led it up to be the largest and most influential church in the Synod of the Columbia, and its power and influence acknowledged throughout the whole of the Pacific Coast; therefore be it

Resolved, That in granting the request of Rev. A. L. Lindsley, D.D., and dissolving the pastoral relation, the Presbytery of Oregon, with gratitude to God, desires to record its satisfaction and appreciation of the pastoral work of Rev. A. L. Lindsley, D. D., and to express its cordial commendation of his industry and power as a preacher and a pastor. We most devoutly pray that the Church may be divinely guided in the choice of a new pastor, who shall take the great responsibilities which our brother is laying down, and carry the work on to still wider and grander achievements. And that our brother now released may, by the blessing of God, be permitted to exert a widening influence in the Master's Kingdom in the high and responsible position to which he has been called. And that this Presbytery pledges to him its most hearty support in his efforts to enlarge and strengthen a sound and reliable school for the training of a Presbyterian ministry for the Pacific Coast.

Remarks of the Commissioners before Presbytery.

At a meeting of the congregation held on the 10th of October, 1886. Hon. H. W. Corbett, Thos. N. Strong and A. W. Stowell were appointed commissioners to notify the Presbytery of the resignation of Dr. Lindsley and of its acceptance by the Church. In presenting this resignation and the resolutions accepting it, which was done October 13th, the commissioners added the following remarks:

Mr. Moderator: In presenting to the reverend body over which you preside the resolutions we have just read, requesting you to accede to Dr. Lindsley's request and dissolve the pastoral relation now existing between him and our church, we feel compelled to more fully express the motives and feeling of our congregation and membership.

Dr. Lindsley came to us on the 31st of July, 1868, over eighteen years ago. At that time we were a young and struggling church with only eighty-seven resident members, burdened with a heavy debt, and strong only in faith and hope. We who were connected with it at that time well remember the situation and the hopes and fears of our little church, as it sent its call to one so far away and so little known to it. We remember, too, the prayers that went up from the church that its choice might be blessed to it and our young community.

It is with a feeling of reverential thankfulness that we now recognize and express how fully the prayers of the church were answered and her hopes realized.

Under Dr. Lindsley's prudent, wise and loving leadership, that little church has grown steadily in spirit, in numbers and in resources until it stands to-day a recognized power for good not only in Portland, but in the world.

Four years and a half ago it numbered four hundred and twelve members. This, with the attendant congregation, overcrowded the old church, and the first migration took place resulting in the formation of Calvary church, which now numbers one hundred and ninety-five members. After that in rapid succession, came the church in East Portland, now numbering ninety-four members; St. John's in North Portland, now numbering fifty-five members; the church in Albina, now numbering forty-nine members; the church at Union Ridge, W. T., now numbering thirty-five members, and the church at Fort Wrangel, now numbering fifty-four members, each of which drew its original membership and resources from our church. For a moment under this heavy drain the old church apparently fell back, and for a short time fear came on its members that it had overleaped itself, but only for a moment. Rapidly and steadily the gaps filled up, and to-day the church has four hundred and twenty-three members, eleven more than it had when it commenced its work of colonizing, and is stronger, and in a better condition financially, morally and spiritually than ever before.

Every one of these younger churches show evidences of vigorous growth, and will, we trust, soon rival in strength and usefulness the mother church.

This alone is a grand work, and yet it is but a portion of what, under the providence of God, Dr. Lindsley has been able to accomplish. Besides paying its own expenses, and acquiring a large and valuable property, the doctor's church, as we may well call it, has during its pastorate raised and expended for outside benevolent purposes the amount of $140,000 of which it has a record, besides thousands more of which no record is possible. Besides this, the Seamen's Home, the Young Men's Christian Association and all kindred enterprises have been helped and fostered. The Indian missions to the Alaskans, Umatillas, Puyallups, Spokanes, Nez Perces and other Indian tribes owe much to Dr. Lindsley and the church over which he presided. Nor were his activities confined to his own church, or its work; during his pastorate he has organized twenty-one churches and dedicated twenty-two, and the church has time and again sent him out on missionary work all over the Northwest and the Pacific coast.

In all this, the church, with a feeling of just pride in its minister and of grave responsibility for the management of the talents committed to its charge, rejoices and takes comfort, and for it, under God, thanks the able, wise and loving pastor who has led it these many years.

Of the original eighty-seven members but twenty-seven now remain with us. A few have gone to other churches, and the great church above has gathered the rest. Those, however, who are alive and all the later members of the church, will always bear in mind more and more tenderly as the years roll on the loving, faithful ministry of Dr. Lindsley. Ever faithful and diligent, there came from him no uncertain sound, and his people to whom he has ministered in storm and in sunshine, in sickness and in health for so long a time, had in him a loving, wise and steadfast counsellor. Under the circumstances, therefore, it was but natural that when the first intimation came that a wider field of usefulness was opening before him, that would involve his separation from his church, that both he and it shrank back. But more and more clearly it became apparent that it was his duty to accept this greater responsibility, and ours to refrain from withholding him from his Master's work.

And so at his earnest request we now release him. We feel that we have no right to hold him back, and with sorrowful hearts we bid him Godspeed in the wider field of usefulness opened before him.

We have much to be thankful for in the past, and this young community has been blessed, in that one so able, pure and influential for good has given so many of his best days. His influence, who shall bound it? Working as he has at the very fountain heads of the history of this portion of the world, he has helped in no slight measure to sweeten and purify its streams forevermore. Only at the grand muster of the resurrection day shall his work be made fully manfest and the jewels of his crown be numbered.

Who shall replace him in this church, congregation and community? We know not, but we can only trust and pray that the God who has so far supported and upheld his great church upon the earth will not leave this little flock untended.

We, therefore, make known to you that, moved by these considerations, we consent this Presbytery should accede to the request of Rev. A. L. Lindsley, D. D., and dissolve the pastoral relation that he now bears to our church, and one and all we prayerfully invoke upon his head the choicest blessings of the prayer-hearing God that he has erved so long and faithfully.

Farewell Discourse.

DELIVERED ON SUNDAY MORNING, NOVEMBER 21, 1886.

Acts XXVI, 15-18. "And I said, who art thou, Lord? And He said, I am Jesus whom thou persecutest. 16. But rise and stand upon thy feet: for I have appeared unto thee for this purpose, to make thee a minister and a witness both of these things which thou has seen, and of those in the which I will appear unto thee; 17. Delivering thee from the people, and from the Gentiles, unto whom now I send thee, 18. To open their eyes, and to turn them from darkness to light, and from the power of Satan unto God, that they may receive forgiveness of sins, and inheritance among them who are sanctified by faith that is in me."

This was St. Paul's ordination to the office of the Gospel ministry, and his apostolic commission, both received from the Head of the Church, not from the hands of men.

Part of his work ended with his life, for he could not transmit it. This was the peculiar service of an Apostle, which no man could assume and no presbytery could confer. This commission appears in these words: "To appoint thee a minister and a witness both of these things which thou hast seen, and of those things in the which I shall appear unto thee."

No man could be an Apostle who had not seen the Lord, and who did not receive his appointment direct from him. But the substance of the Apostle's office belongs to the ministry which Christ ordained to continue to the end of time. I will read the words which apply to the preacher, evangelist and pastor:

8

Acts 26:16, 18. "I have appeared unto thee for this purpose * * * to open the eyes of them to whom I send thee, and to turn them from darkness to light, and from the power of Satan unto God, that they may receive forgiveness of sins, and the inheritance among them that are sanctified by faith in me".

We understand by this commission the full work of the gospel ministry, as it lay in the mind of its divine founder: it was appointed to convey the knowledge of salvation to the helpless and lost and guilty sons of men.

The sincere minister opens the eyes of the blind who are lost in the wilderness of sin, and are therefore helpless: to guide them out of the darkness to Him who said:

John 8:12. "I am the light of the world; he that followeth me shall not walk in the darkness, but shall have the light of life."

In guiding them to the Fountain of Light, he rescues them from the Evil One who is lying in ambush to deceive and destroy; he brings them into the presence of the God of infinite love, that they may receive the forgiveness of their sins and be made his children by adoption, and joint-heirs with the well-beloved Son of the inheritance which is, reserved in Heaven; and all of this series of unspeakable gifts and blessings abounding within us and around us through the riches of grace in Christ Jesus, and dependent upon faith in Him.

The Apostle exercised his sacred gifts with supreme devotion. "He was not disobedient to the heavenly vision" when he showed them that they should repent and turn to God*.

He was a man of great learning, and a lawyer of rising eminence; but he laid all his resources under contribution to set forth the salvation of the Cross and the glory of the Redeemer.

The thought of his own inablility to save men kept him humble, yet the grandeur of his theme made him soar to the skies. He caught the fire from the altar, and brought it down to kindle devotion in human hearts. He said of himself:

*Acts 26:19, 20.

9

Eph. 3:8, 9. "Unto me who am less than the least of all saints, is this grace given, that I should preach * * * * the unsearchable riches of Christ; and to make all men see what is the fellowship of the mystery which from the beginning of the world hath been hid in God."

But within all that this Apostle ever said or wrote, stood character; and this gave weight to what he said, helped by the power of God. His talents, his legal training, his eloquence, all his gifts and graces, were less influential than the character which he possessed. And we find in the following words the key to it all:

2 Cor. 1:12. "Our rejoicing is this, the testimony of our conscience, that in simplicity and godly sincerity, not with fleshly wisdom but by the grace of God, we have had our conversation in the world."

This explains his life. It shows us what the principles were that regulated his conversation in the Church and in the world. He is showing us, therefore, just what the character of a true preacher should be. His conscience is enlightened by a knowledge of God's will and he obeys its dictates. Therefore he has the testimony of his conscience.

When this faculty has its supreme place, it moulds a state of mind called conscientiousness; and this is essential to personal worth. It should rest like the pillars of a noble structure upon the granite foundations of character; and then they will lift aloft the glory and the beauty of the whole.

Then conscientiousness will appear in simplicity; it has no time to dally with error or temptation. For conscience dwells in light, and rebukes duplicity in speech, conduct, heart and mind.

Another word for simplicity is singleness; and our Saviour said: "If thine eye be single, thy whole body shall be full of light."

This the Apostle meant when he said, "This one thing I do," * as he pressed with singleness of aim toward the mark which was not double. The simplicity of his character found expression when he said, "I determined not to know anything among you save Jesus

Phil. 3:13.

Christ and him crucified." He it was who also spoke of the simplicity that is in Christ, and he labored to make men rejoice in the testimony of their own conscience that they might please God rather than men.

To this virtue the Apostle added sincerity, which, perhaps, relates to his speech; being very desirous to speak the truth as it is in Jesus. And it was godly sincerity. For salvation was so great a blessing and upon which hung the weight of souls, that the Apostle aimed with all his self-conviction to show that God was infinitely sincere in providing it.

These admirable qualities the Apostle rejoiced in. He was in labors abundant, in perils often, and in temptations great; from all which he might have escaped if he had run his career by the maxims of "fleshly wisdom." But now he rejoiced that he had run it "by the grace of God," and had persuaded multitudes to follow him.

This great Apostle's conscience testified to his faithfulness. So clear was this testimony that he rejoiced in it also. And in this view, it is very suggestive that he could say to the Ephesian elders:

Acts 20:27. "I have not shunned to declare unto you the whole counsel of God."

All preachers can safely follow his example with wisdom from on high to guide them in the selection of topics which belong to God's counsel, and in the treatment of them. For some of his counsel is very mysterious, and bewildering to ordinary hearers, and to young people. I have thought it was not wise to dwell much upon them. Such are the doctrines of the entrance of sin, and of the election of a part of the race to salvation; and the doctrine of everlasting punishment I have chosen to treat as a logical deduction from the Law of God which, being broken and set at naught, must exact the penalty unless the Law-giver vacates the Judgment-seat and renounces his sovereignty, and flings his sceptre into the hands of Satan.

Upon this threshold we have aimed to show that the Gospel is an expedient of mercy suspending the law of retribution which prevails in all the Universe, in order that during the reprieve, the terms of pardon might be considered and accepted, so that when the Gospel stands no longer in the way, and the Law flashes back its awful penalty, the rescued ones should come forth from the final conflagration without the smell of fire upon the imperishable robes of their acquired righteousness.

And how did they acquire the righteousness that triumphed over the penalty? A prophet exclaims:

Isaiah 63:1. "Who is this that cometh from Edom, with dyed garments from Bozrah, this that is glorious in his apparel, traveling in the greatness of his strength?"

Listen for his answer, as he sinks the mountains of transgression to make a highway for our God,

"I that speak in righteousness, mighty to save!"

The coming of God manifest in human nature, his teachings, his miracles, his sufferings, his resurrection, ascension and intercession, his everlasting kingdom and glory—ah, these are the themes which I have delighted to dwell upon, together with the nature of faith, repentance, justification and sanctification.

I have honored the Holy Spirit, as administrator of the kingdom of Christ on earth during his bodily presence in Heaven, especially to teach the world the guilt and misery and desert of sin ; to persuade us to believe ; to show us our pardon ; to transform us into the spirit of adoption ; to incline us to lead a holy life, after Christ's example, and to discharge our duty to the Church, and to the world ; and to enable us to persevere, that we may never renounce what he has taught us; to anoint our eyes that we may seek another country, even a heavenly, while our lives are hid with Christ in God.

This is what being born again means ; this is being renewed in the spirit of the mind ; this is being created in the righteousness and holiness of the truth after the image of Him that creates us in Christ unto good works "which God before ordained that we should walk in them.'"

The preacher who proclaims these truths is sowing the seeds of character that shall abide forever. They shall bear the fruit of the Spirit which is life everlasting.

And character is the essence of life. All that is really permanent about us is personal worth ; and all that is worth saving about us is the fruit of virtue—the goodness we have encouraged ; the sufferings we have relieved : the fallen we have lifted up; the tempted we have rescued.—all the outflowing of the perennial spring which is hidden in the rock. character.

Character is built up with principle, which is the granite laid in the wall. The application of principle is the cement which binds the whole together. These principles must be moral and religious. No principles should be wrought into character which are not permanent and which will not survive the ordeal of death. No character which is destitute of moral principle can endure the strain of our common life; and no morality is strong enough to endure it which is without the help of God. Religion, therefore, must be inwrought with the fiber of character. It alone can reinforce natural virtue, and give both light and decision to moral questions as they arise, and thus the immortal powers are trained for prompt and efficient action in this world, and prepared for higher service in the kingdom of God.

I have not thought that the best way to build up character was to keep up a continual assault upon particular sins and fashionable follies; but that the best way to remove them was to inculcate the opposite virtues. And so to commend the Christian graces in their beauty and excellency, that they would supplant the inclinations of corrupt or polished lusts. It is written: "Walk in the Spirit, and ye shall not fulfil the lusts of the flesh." *

Inspire the soul with the holier motive, and it will press forward "toward the mark of the high calling," "forgetting the things that are behind and reaching forth." When character is established, restraint is pleasure and self-denial sweet.

Then character is growth. It is invisible only as a purposeful life reveals it. It is just Christ being formed within. All reforms, all culture, all personal worth become permanent, just as they become parts of character; and this is to grow in grace and in loving acquaintance and fellowship with the Lord Jesus Christ. This is the highest attainment of our nature. It begins with being born anew, and ends in likeness to Christ. It is the scriptural approach to the Christian

Gal. 5:16.

ideal. It is the answer to the Apostle's prayer, and the end of his labors, "Christ within the hope of glory." *

This growth the ministry is ordained to inculcate and superintend. The pastors whom God declared to be after his own heart, are those that "feed the people with knowledge and understanding," and Paul (Eph. 4,) says the design of our Lord in ordaining them was the "perfecting of the saints, the edifying of·the body of Christ." The chief work of the ministry, therefore, is to build up the people into a strong and manly religious character; to establish them in the doctrines of grace; and to guide them in sanctified efforts for the salvation of a perishing world.

Such is the controlling and strenuous aim of the ministry; and I have spared nothing that could help me to gain it, for your sakes. A few words will explain my preparation for it, and give you an insight into the current of thought and devotion upon which I have caused you to float in sermons and lectures and prayers.

I was early devoted to the Christian ministry; but my studies in various branches of the liberal education increased my thirst for universal knowledge and led me to prepare myself for another pursuit. I thought I could not acquire a comprehensive education if I should follow the sacred profession; and this caused me to waver, especially as I had an inextinguishable thirst both for literary studies and scientific investigations. And over this vast area of human knowledge, I delighted to push philosophical speculation to its utmost verge.

But I could not banish from my thoughts that the most comprehensive culture could be employed in vindicating the ways of God to man, and that the brightest flower and fruit of such an education would only bring the richer contributions to the altar of consecration to Him by whom the worlds were made, the Lord of angels, the Maker and Redeemer of mankind.

And to this conclusion was I brought at last; and I think that it is worthy of mention now as giving you a substantial reason for my manifold efforts to convince you that the whole system of the Universe

Col. 1:27.

seen and unseen, and all the philosophical theories that have ever been broached among men, and all the real attainments of knowledge, can be followed up to their meeting-place of perfect harmony in the Lord Jesus Christ.

I have entered the conflict between faith and reason, science and religion, not as a combatant, but as a peacemaker capable by my own studies to lay my hand upon the one with an inflexible grasp, and by the grace of God upon the other, with the clearest convictions of the truths revealed in Holy Scripture, centering in the gift of eternal life to the sincere followers of the Son of God.

I think that I was led by the Spirit of God who the Saviour said should guide his disciples into all the truth, to dedicate myself anew to the ministry after having acquired these comprehensive and saving views of God's relation to the Universe, and of man's relation to God. All consistent lines of thought lead again to the center, Christ.

A desire to exhibit the grounds for our faith in Christ, as the author of the only religion for the world, has always been controlling and overwhelming. I have never been able to reach the top of the high argument to my own satisfaction; and sometimes I have painfully felt that I have not made the deep impression upon my hearers which the subject deserved,—but which the advocate was unable to make.

No expression can compass the exalted nature of the subject; and they feel this most who have most tried to express it.

Yet, after all, if only a few are deeply impressed with the grandeur of the atonement and the efficacy of the Christian faith, it were enough to reward the utmost endeavors of the preacher to make the doctrines plain.

Mind rules our country. The thinking of master minds in one age often becomes the popular opinions of the next. This transfusion is effected by the diligence of the earnest thinkers who perceive what civilization needs to expand it as well as to urge it onward.

The same is true of the progress of the gospel. A few spirits gifted with such prophecies and gathering around central thoughts, push them forward into the midst, and compel the attention of similar spirits who enlist in the cause. The circumference widens as new circles of influence are created, like the watch-fires that illuminate a vast encampment at night.

God directs the thinkers of one age who are to impress their ideas upon a succeeding one. They are not always conscious that they are moving under the direction of God's spirit.

Saul was among the prophets, but he acted contrary to the will of God. In the history of the race many a Saul appears, and some of them do not know that God could say to them, "for this purpose I have raised thee up."

In this manner we explain the well-known fact that writers who disregard the revealed will of God, often outline improvement in governments and reforms in society, which are taken up by the Church in process of time; and made to do efficient work in the cause of the world's final redemption.

This is only a further proof that all things in Heaven and on earth, and under the earth, shall contribute to the glory of Christ and the triumph of his cause.

There are ministers in all denominations who are qualified to occupy these exalted outlooks and survey the whole scene with a prophet's ken. They conduct from every spring the streams that flow toward the great fountain of human cleansing and enlightenment.

While I feel like one of old who wrote that he was one of the least of all saints, I have also been most keenly alive to the unspeakable importance of gathering from the broad field of truth in nature, philosophy and history, whatever could help "to make all men see what is the fellowship of the mystery which, from the beginning of the world, hath been hid in God."

You perceive that the "mystery" was to be explained, and therefore no longer remained hidden. And it was not to be for the benefit of a few, but there was to be a fellowship in it, for God was no respecter of persons, and the Apostle wrote "to make *all* men see," and seeing to enter into the fellowship. And therefore we are penetrated and possessed with the inextinguishable desire to make the men of this generation see it ; and each in our allotted sphere to gather the resources of argument and illustration in order to pour the whole, like tides of living light, upon the entire community. This will impart the most valuable knowledge to the general mind, and incline it to apprehend the truth of Christianity; and thereby prevent or cure the skepticism which is born of ignorance and bred by the vague assumptions of one-sided philosophers, cavernous researches, and fossilized speculation. When this is made to appear, evangelical Christianity will compel respect, and the minds of the young and uninformed will not be so constantly assailed by false assumptions.

And so it happened that the student who had loved the classic literatures, and looked with delight upon the capabilities of his own mother-tongue, and had gone forth into the domain of nature, and read the story of the rocks and rebuilt the fossils into living forms; and anon penetrated the sidereal universe in an ecstacy of intellectual fervor; now turned with the warm glow of spiritual devotion to behold the light which guided the wise men to Bethlehem, and thereafter shown with increasing lustre as it rose, bidding fair to illuminate the whole world of mankind.

Now it must be apparent to every thoughtful mind that the aim of this culture should be ever single and prominent. The aim will admit of no division or diversion. It should be no less than the Master's, who came to redeem mankind by making them new creatures. As He surveyed the scene which ended with the Cross, He exclaimed, "How am I straightened till it be accomplished!"

But the renewal was not to be accomplished by any worldly means, or any intellectual or scientific end. Culture could not do it. Philosophy was weak when it claimed to be strongest. And the soul of the most eminent in any literary or artistic pursuit is just as much lost without a humble trust in a divine Redeemer, as if he had never been translated from the lowliest cot of the child of ignorance or bondage.

The minister who fails to do this, fails in efficiency as a preacher. He has missed his mark, and missed it most widely when he aimed too high; for the mass of his hearers are persons who come to be persuaded by the voice of the preacher, craving a knowledge of the truth, indeed, but longing to have it conveyed in a warm and sympathetic manner, and expressed with simplicity and sincerity, as the fruitage of his devout studies, and the pulsations of his heart.

And this gives the occupant of the pulpit his real power; which must be replenished by a continual resort to the sources of divine knowledge, while he stands abreast of all the substantial progress of the times, and turns it to the account of the welfare of his fellow-creatures for time and eternity.

The ministry is not and must not be exclusively confined to college-bred men. There are preachers without the advantages of learning who are endowed with gifts of nature and grace which enable them to bring many souls into the kingdom. With thanks to God who raises up such men to rebuke the pride of high culture and remind the ministry with whom the residue of power dwells, it must still be apparent that intellectual training cannot be dispensed with. The man in any profession who is able to influence his contemporaries has *staying power*, because he knows where his resources are and how to use them, whether they are stored like securities in a bank-vault, and the possessor holding the secret of the combination lock; or whether they lie upon the open field of nature, and the searcher one who has learned how to interrogate her; or whether they are the thoughts of the world's thinkers which he has studied, or the works of the world's builders which he has surveyed. A man cannot cultivate his powers too highly to serve Christ and his fellow men. Such is the view of the most eminent Christians in all denominations.

But a great danger rises at this point. It is the danger of making a breach between the educated ministry and the unevangelized masses. It is the danger that exists in all stages of culture or education. The classes drift apart by natural tendency. But whether a breach is made between the educated preacher and the untrained masses of the people, depends upon the spirit of the man. The cause of Christ demands the enlarged education. Modern progress demands it. We must have educated ministers; and they must not drift away from the people, nor let the masses drift away from them.

The preventive is, not in abridging true culture, but in educating the people to relish discourse which combines nature and revelation, and works over both in such a way as to purify, console, enlighten and edify every one in the congregation, young and old, and to unite all in the bonds of sacred fellowship and the hope of everlasting life; and all being made to sit together in heavenly places in Christ Jesus.

To make a sermon like this, a man need not parade any of his scholarship. He keeps his machinery out of sight, like the great motive power in the steamship that holds on her way through storm or calm. Just such a demonstration should every sermon be, inviting all passengers to a hospitable entertainment and a safe voyage.

If the masses do not come to the church, let the minister take the church to the masses. To do this he will find all the discipline and scholarship which he can acquire available, and every energy of his being must be made auxiliary to labor and to serve. He will give nerve and direction to associations outside of his own congregation in schools and colleges, in salutary reforms, in special missions to the outcast and exposed, in secular charities, and in all Christ-like ways; and he will employ the press to give wider information, casting the weight of all his influence upon the pathway of mankind toward the coming of our Lord Jesus Christ. *

Profoundly convinced of the sin and want of human hearts and of the all-sufficiency of Christ to relieve them, the utterances of this pulpit have dwelt upon the soul and its salvation, the Saviour and His redeeming mercy, the adopting love of God shed abroad in the heart by the Holy Spirit, the transforming influence of faith in the unseen, and the sure realizations of hope anchored in the oath-bound promises. The light which shines upon the pulpit has radiated to the outer rim of human interests; for nothing that concerns our race should be foreign to the pulpit. Rulers and statesmen are busy with the affairs of nations; but the progress of Christian undertakings at home and abroad is a more absorbing study than any other that can occupy the mind of the world.

---

* "It may be glorious to write   [three
  Thoughts that shall glad the two or
  High souls like those far stars that come
  Once in a century: [in sight

But better far it is to speak
  The simple words that now and then
  Shall waken a new nature in the weak
  And sinful sons of men."

Amidst these multiplied claims the church and its ordinances must ever stand foremost. It is "the church of the living God, the pillar and ground of the truth." All things must be made tributary to its advancement and its glory. The minister standing at its altars, sows the seed on fields of various promise, cultivates it, rising early and working late; then waits for the harvest. He shall reap as he has sown. "He that soweth bountifully shall also reap bountifully." Sometimes the fruitage comes from heathen lands, sometimes from the sea. But what harvest is so delightful as the ingathering of souls from the families composing the congregation? When the strong man brings the vigor of his days to the altar of dedication—when the faithful woman adds the crown of godliness to her virtues—it is bright evidence of the power of divine truth upon the conscience and the heart. This is to many the best proof that can be afforded of the efficacy of the Gospel working its silent convictions in the mind, and its transformations in the spirit: and thus the harvest after much tillage appears. But to a pastor's heart no sight is so cheering as the groups of children that yield to the claims of the Son of God, and being led by His Spirit devote their young being to His service. No garden is so promising as this, and none so beautiful. It should be cultivated with increasing diligence by parents and pastors and teachers. When this fruit is gathered in, the first intention of the church operates harmoniously, for the saints young and old are only children of God always growing up to the fullness of the stature of Christ. The times demand the strenuous efforts of pastors and people to bring the children to decision. Impressions must be followed up. The greatest encouragement should be given to pastors not only at home but in the Sunday school and in the church. Sermons to children should be welcomed by the presence of those for whom they are prepared, and if constraint is needed, should it not be employed?—wisely, indeed, but persistently and affectionately, deeming but little gained until the end is secured. Earlier than ever before are the children drawn away from the father's tutelage and the mother's tender care. If they hear not the voice of the good Shepherd now, what hope should we entertain that they will hear it when the world's clamors fill their ears?

I have labored in revivals in which much the largest proportion of converts were children and youth. And no sight has blest the pastor's eyes so beautiful and even glorious as when he gazed upon the innocent faces and into the uplifted eyes of children standing here and taking upon themselves the vows which their parents assumed on their behalf; and mingled with them children of unconverted parents made welcome in the fold.

Our joy abounds when Christianity wins victories upon the fields of conflict with various forms of hostility. We are deeply moved in the advance of salutary reforms when stoutly contested positions have been carried, or turned to account of human welfare : but the church's embrace of the young are the arms of a mother thrown around her offspring with a grasp that never relaxes : and in that embrace is the transmission of a new enlivening of every grace, and confirming the character that it may be developed into symmetry and consistency after the pattern of the child Jesus. O honored mother! whose arms are full of them,—they shall be your glory and your defence as the years press on! They shall learn Christ without the friction of evil passions, without the dislocations of worldly habits, without the clash of opposing interests, or the compromises of trade which is conducted contrary to the commandments of God, or the purity, truth and charity of religion. These are the shields of the mighty. These are the panoply of the church, and the guardians of the nation. They are also the purest gems in the pastor's crown ; and their lustre shall brighten as the ages roll.

In approaching the severance of my official relation to this church, I deem it becoming to state some facts and offer some reflections.

Nineteen years have passed away since the call was addressed to me. Although I declined it then, its renewal prevailed, and I first saw this place eighteen years ago last July. I immediately assumed my pastoral work. I hope I shall be pardoned if I speak of myself at the end of my ministry among you, as my motive is not now liable to be misunderstood, especially as I have with almost total silence abstained from references to myself in public or private.

I had invitations to churches in eastern cities and San Francisco ; but I was led to accept your call in consequence of what I believed to be the dictate of Divine Providence in connection with my own inclinations; for I had always felt a prevailing disposition to devote my life to missionary work ; and I regarded Portland as the center of a vast missionary field. I will frankly say that Portland, considered by itself at that time, was not sufficient. I was bound to use the powers that God had given me and which had been improved by some degree of culture and experience, upon the widest field that I could compass by His grace; and after a full consideration of this locality and the territory which stretched out from it in every direction, the circumstances which determined my mind were peculiarly impressive and providential. They formed an epoch in my life. They were decisive. They led me to embark in the greater work which I believe God assigned to me in this extensive region of our country. There were but four Presbyterian ministers in active service, and many fields were already white to the harvest. Yet no laborers were coming. I could not withhold my voice, nor pen, nor presence, and I cast all my powers and resources into the work.

In the progress of my ministry I have had to encounter criticisms, and I gave them most respectful consideration. But I could not forget that when adverse opinion came to me, it was not authority which must be obeyed, but as a subject for serious examination and prayer. A little more grace and a little more confiding in the pastor, or willingness to let him act out his convictions, would have in many instances made his work easier and his heart merrier; but I acted on the principle of going on with the work of the Lord, whether aided by many or by few, in the belief that the cause would grapple the hearts and consciences of some of my people, if not all, and the Lord's work would prosper ; and in this I have not been wholly disappointed.

During these years the temporalities of the church have been ably conducted. The trustees have maintained its credit by meeting all obligations, sometimes largely at their own expense. They have carried into its business transactions the maxims which regulate secular affairs among prudent managers.

To the Session, as constituted at different periods, and to individuals composing it, this congregation is indebted for prudent and prayerful oversight. As advisers and fellow-laborers with the pastor, they have ever been ready to perform any service for the advancement of the cause. They have cheerfully given time and means required of all loyal Presbyterians when elevated to office by their brethren. They have sustained the burden both of insight and oversight of the flock ; they have given indispensable support to the pastor ; they have upheld the dignity and honor of the church in the works of benevolence, and before the world. Their influence has been felt and their recommendations respected throughout the entire congregation. As many of these services must be given unknown to the congregation, I cannot refrain from saying these few words.

The payment of the debt on the church-building, and the collection of the Memorial Fund amounting to $1,427, mark a decided epoch in the contributions for benevolent objects. That payment set us free from the necessity of consuming our resources upon ourselves; and the raising of a fund which was set forth in the pulpit with great fullness and at different times, made us acquainted with the aims and methods for the propagation of the Gospel pursued in the Presbyterian Church through its General Assembly, and created a sympathy in its objects which had not before existed, or which we could not indulge to any considerable extent. Since that happy clearance our growth in the grace of giving has been marked. The contributions have been greatly increased by a few prosperous givers ; the donations of the many have not changed so much as they should have done.

Reminiscences crowd upon me which would occupy hours to describe. I can touch only upon prominent points as I go along. I could speak of munificent gifts to charities, education and churches; and I disparage none of them while I pause to speak of one gift as the outgrowth of Christian beneficence which is worthy of a very prominent place in the memorials of this church. It also shows the foresight of a comprehensive survey of the greatest need of the church on the whole Pacific Coast, and indicates the enlargement of the devout liberality which hears the voice from heaven, " Freely ye have received, freely

give." The donor is not present; and I therefore take the liberty to
refer to an appropriation of property which is so well worthy of mention on the occasion of my translation from this charge to the professorship in our Theological School.*

The Ladies' Sewing Society was a power in the church which de-
serves grateful remembrance. Its services on the church property and in
keeping down the debt, were simply invaluable. It helped other
churches also ; and one of its most signal efforts was the purchase of
Westminster Chapel for our mission school.

Living streams of beneficence have flowed from the Sunday school,
which were like incense offered on the altar, acceptable to God as his
children's praise.

Special appeals for worthy objects have been worthily met ; and
there are instances in which your aid gave the efficient encouragement
that led to success—a wise method which entices others to participate
in building up a common benefaction. The Home for the Friendless is

---

*The following letter addressed to the donor will show your pastor's view of
the signal gift which has drawn after it the donations of many that might otherwise have never been devoted to this cause. The letter is as follows:

PORTLAND, OREGON, March 31, 1886.

W. S. LADD, ESQ.

My Dear Brother:—I cannot refrain from expressing to you in this formal manner the broad appreciation which all well-informed men must feel in view of your
contribution to the cause of Theological Education. It is unexampled on this coast,
and seldom paralleled on any shore. The devotement of it to the cause of ministerial culture and equipment is really a provision for general education, for it has
ever been observed that an educated ministry is the support and exponent of education among the people.

Your magnificent gift will be fruitful in other ways. It will be an incentive to
men of property and draw forth benefactions which might not otherwise see the
light.

But the timeliness of it is a stroke of foresight which has an immediate bearing upon ministerial training on this coast. It makes provision for it, and thereby
invites pious young men to prepare themselves for a theological course.

I cannot suppress the consideration that through this instrumentality you will
be preaching the everlasting Gospel long after your own lips shall be silent here:
though I pray God that you may live long to enjoy the consciousness of current
successes following your liberal and well-considered endowments and charities.

With highest respect, I remain your pastor and friend.

a joy-inspiring example that sheds the smiles of children made happy upon the hearts of their benefactors. Nor is it unworthy of mention that the first missions and schools in Alaska were begun in this congregation ; and the means and materials for erecting the first American house of worship built in that territory, together with the first missionaries, were provided here. Thanks be to God for His unspeakable gift !

Your Christian labors I cannot pass by without comment, lest I should seem to underrate them. Your liberality is not confined to your own branch of the church universal, neither are your labors. Some of these disciples are toilers and leaders in every good word and work. You have also struggled along with your spiritual guides to replenish our own church under the repeated strain of organizing colonies ; and the pastor, occupying a higher post of observation, has with devout thankfulness noted the loyalty and zeal which animated you as our ranks closed up after the departure of each colony. Pastor and elders and people sent them forth with help and benediction ; and then with unabated courage labored to restore the equipoise and renew our strength, without abridging our labors or contributions in behalf of the common cause. Systematic giving as God has prospered you, would greatly increase your benefactions and your spirit of devotion. Steps have been considered in the Session which will lead to a better plan and richer returns into the treasuries of the Lord, when you shall have entered your new house of worship.

Christian women were the founders of this church. Through their labors and persuasions this site was bought and paid for, and this temple built. A few only of that devoted band remain in its communion on earth : but many more are treading in their footsteps ; and I should do violence to my own convictions if I should fail to commend to your most respectful regard the Order of Deaconesses, whose unostentatious services the pastor gratefully acknowledges ; and with the hope that it will never be disbanded, I quote the inspired commendation, " Help those women who labored with me in the gospel, * * * and with other my fellow laborers, whose names are in the book of life."

A long cherished desire of the pastor's heart was at last gratified in the formation of the young people's Association for mutual improvement, for cultivating acquaintance with strangers, and for any departments of usefulness which are timely and consistent. Its meetings have made very favorable impressions on my mind ; and its donations have been peculiarly valuable. It is cultivating in a congenial atmosphere the Christian graces which are most social and attractive at a time when sinful amusements are most alluring : it is strengthening character in all that is noble, discreet, sincere and manly, a consistent rebuke of the irreligious and profligate spirit that is so widely prevalent among young men. The expediency of such a society is beyond debate ; the ends in view and the outcome of its influence may wisely be left to the counsels of experience and the guidance of the Holy Spirit. Informed by such maxims and chastened by growth in grace, this Association will be a harmonious development of the church school, a luxuriant branch of the parent tree.

I speak of the Mission to the Chinese chiefly to commend it to your sympathy and help. It is the outgrowth of repeated undertakings on their behalf which exacted funds and self-denial borne by a few. These children of the continent opposite to our coast are the victims of a civilization which stiffened into its existing forms like a frozen sea ages before the Christian era began ; and in many things they are children yet. They appreciate words of kindness ; and some of them who are brethren in Christ wonder at the treatment they receive from their fellow-heirs in the household of faith. I remind you that some of the members of your own communion, one of them a Chinese woman, are among the most devoted missionaries to these peculiar people. They are going with their Master outside of the camp bearing His reproach. Let them not bear it alone.

The common tendency to run in grooves and survey with complacency the motions of the machinery, has been discountenanced by the watchman on these towers. The agencies of the congregation have not been sped on steel or golden rails. Our chariot of salvation built in heaven was wafted down on angels' wings which overshadow it still ; and the breath of God has urged it along the highways and hedges of this world. It has borne its banners in the front of battle against every form of wickedness, adjusting itself to every phase of the conflict ; and its trumpet has given no uncertain sound, proclaiming the fullness of salvation to all classes and conditions of men on the land and on the waters, * and at the outlook of the sea.†

The change of location will bring changes into the congregation. They will not bring dangers but blessings, if you act in the spirit of fellowship and love. But your prosperity will require continued missionary work. In nothing will your welcome to my successor be more grateful to him than in the spirit of co-operation for the edification of the church, and your missionary zeal in building up the congregation. This is the two-fold task which God assigns to every church in these days.

The changes which take place in the congregations of all growing cities, are marked and emphasized in Portland. Immigration, fluctuations of business, and growth of the city, make social and domestic life changeable ; and the congregation fluctuates. If it were not for some of the pioneers who are the pillars of this church, it would have lost its identity. Only twenty-seven of the members who welcomed me, remain. Of the others who are now on its roll, and on the rolls of its colonies, much the larger proportion has been gathered from the ranks of strangers.

And besides this there is a revolution going on in society. I repeat, the drift is away from the churches; and to catch a share of it as it floats by, we must open the doors wide, and pilot the strangers in ! Then, with sympathy, confidence and fellowship you will win them and their children to Christ and His cause.

That church is doomed to arctic apathy and death by collapse, which does not replenish its strength and multiply its adherents by accessions from the world. The nature of Christianity is aggressive. All its equipment is adapted to growth. All its armor is forged for the combat and the march, and none for retreat. We are soldiers of the Cross. We are laborers together with God. Our line of work runs parallel to His, or is one with it. Every church is a lighthouse amidst

---

* The Seamen's Friend Society. † The Holman Chapel at Ilwaco.

surrounding darkness. It is commanded to let its light so shine before
men that our Father in Heaven may be glorified.

In reviewing these years of associated effort, it becomes us devoutly
to acknowledge the benignant Providence that has watched over this
congregation, the Angel of the covenant who hath guided and guarded
it, and the indwelling Spirit who hath fostered and developed its
graces in every state of interior growth and visible activity. The God
of all our mercies has dealt very graciously with us, notwithstanding
our shortcomings and infirmities ; and we are this day a monument of
His forgiving and restoring grace.

He has also guided many choice spirits into our communion, and
made it the gate of Heaven to some of them whose memories we
cherish with reverent regard, awaiting the recognition of friends when
God shall wipe the tears from every eye. He has preserved others
upon whose faces we look to-day who occupy the same places for long
years in Session, trusteeship and in choir, in prayer-meeting and Sunday school and in benevolent societies. The spirit of co-operation
which exists between the Session and the people, is a cause of thankfulness and a promise of greater growth and blessing.

Amidst these realities the pastor ventures to exclaim, "Ye are my
witnesses." So Christ said, so the Apostle wrote. So every minister
of the Gospel is entitled to say. But it is a solemn searching appeal to
the most sacred influences ever exerted by one spirit upon other spirits.
Yet I have really no other decisive test of my ministry. For a pastor's
success does not depend upon the number of conversions visible and en-
rolled, though that is one mark which should not be wanting. But no
real conversion can be attributed to any human being as the direct or
efficient cause. The minister's duty is to persuade men to seek recon-
ciliation to God ; but the Holy Spirit alone can change the heart. The
crucial test of pastoral efficiency is in the culture of souls that profess
to be converted. He calls sinners to repentance, and builds up the
saints on their most holy faith.

During these years I have been doing this two-fold work among you.
And I take a survey of this church with a kind of satisfaction which I

believe is not inconsistent with humility. The Lord knows with what degree of singleness of aim I have executed the work of a builder among you : but I am allowed to say in sincerity that I have kept nothing back that could profit you : and God knoweth how blamelessly and carefully I have endeavored to walk among you. "I have coveted no man's silver or gold or apparel." Had gain been my object I would have chosen another field and a richer investment. But I determined to know nothing among you save Jesus Christ and Him crucified. "Ye are my glory and my joy." I have earnestly sought to save you from the imbecility of sentimental religiousness, by transferring the promises, hopes and affections of Christianity into an active and consistent life.

It has been your pastor's happy lot, as some of you have often said, to help you by his prayers and his teaching. If you have ever learned from him something about yourselves which it was important for you to know,—if he has understood your deeper wants and your unsatisfied feelings and comforted you, he has not done it by any chilling speculations, but by bringing to your remembrance what our Lord has spoken, and what His most faithful followers have felt in your circumstances. If he has helped you to realize that there is a higher life than the one which society is following,—if he has led you to contemplate another world than the one you are wont to see, and to read therein your own title to a heavenly mansion ; the recollection will be to him a source of pure consolation when he is far away, and to you the guide and fountain of everlasting joy.

May I not, as I go away from your sight, rest in the belief that I have opened the way to diviner life than you had ever experienced before ; that I have encouraged some of you who were desponding, answered the enquiring, comforted the sorrowing, guided the baffled, and strengthened the weak and tempted ; in short, if I have said or done something to give you a clearer insight into the indwelling of the Spirit that God has shed abroad in your hearts to bear witness with your spirits that you are his beloved children ? Then I entreat you to cast a loving thought towards him whom you shall hear no more in this place, and pray that the true words he has spoken may dwell in you

richly in all wisdom, until the heavenly vision shall brighten with un-
fading lustre what you see dimly here.

> * I need not be missed, if my life has been bearing
> (As its summer and autumn move silently on)
> The bloom, and the fruit, and the seed of the season,—
> I shall be remembered by what I have done.
>
> I need not be missed if another succeeds me,
> To reap down the fields which in spring I have sown :
> He who plowed and who sowed is not missed by the reaper,
> He is only remembered by what he has done.
>
> Not myself, but the truth that in life I have spoken,
> Not myself, but the seed that in life I have sown,
> Shall pass on to ages—all about me forgotten,
> Save the truth I have spoken, and things I have done.
>
> Up and away like the dew of the morning,
> That soars from the earth to its home in the sun ;
> So let me steal away gently and lovingly,
> Only remembered by what I have done.

The review of any ministry is very solemn. How much more so
when it has been extended through half the average life of a generation! It is the longest Presbyterian pastorate on the Pacific Coast ;
and there can be but few as long in any denomination. It has had
imperfections and omissions ; and none can know so well as the pastor
how they have been deplored ; and with what anxiety he has aimed
and striven to avoid them. But one thing is certain—not one of these
mistakes was founded in intention or unfaithfulness. The appearance
of mistake has sometimes been the means which God has blessed to
the furtherance of ends which lay very near the pastor's heart ; but he
thought it was wise to say nothing after it was past. Let it go. Forget the things that are behind. Let God "require that which is past."

I have often seen the promise verified in my own experience :
Psalm 37; 5, 6: "Commit thy way unto the Lord ; trust also in Him
* * * and He shall bring forth thy righteousness as
the light, and thy judgment as the noonday."

I prize among the best gifts of God's Spirit the grace of forgiveness.

* HORATIUS BONAR.

There is not one who has misunderstood me or misconstrued my motives, that I have not sincerely forgiven, or whom I would not serve with all my heart. And if I have been so unfortunate as to have given to any one just occasion for taking offence, I do not know it. Or, if I have ever injured any one, I will gladly make restitution to the utmost of my power. We shall soon appear at the judgment-seat. But it is not a human bar. It is the last tribunal; for the dead, small and great, shall stand before God.

I leave you a strong, compact, united congregation. Your speedy recovery from the recurrent strain of departing detachments is a token of God's favor, and a prophecy of your growth and expansion. To fulfill it will require enlarged efforts, generous appropriations, and resolute devotement. There remains much talent in the church which should find employment on lines within the benevolent work of the congregation, or in the parts of the city which will be left quite unoccupied by us when your removal shall have taken place. I remind you of the importance of the section of the city around the Mariner's Home—a cause and a region which have peculiar claims upon us. My acquaintance with the spiritual destitution of that large part of the city, and my sympathy for seamen (the most neglected and yet the most useful pioneers of the world's material progress), have heretofore led me to urge these claims with pertinacity, under a deep sense of the church's responsibility. The full embrace of the opportunity will yield the richest missionary harvest of the church. "Let no man take thy crown." Under a renewed pledge of obedience, let every disciple, and especially the unemployed, inquire, "Lord, what wilt thou have me to do?" and then go about some Christian work to prove your sincerity. Under clear convictions of duty I have sometimes labored alone, partly because "the King's business" required dispatch, and the discussion of measures might interpose a fatal delay; and partly because the work was new, and I preferred to bear alone the risk of an untried experiment. Such cases will occur in every active life. It is time you were doing something more than you have done: "for the night is far spent, the day is at hand."

God will guide your conscience; then leave to Him to accept your work and vindicate your motives. Let this conviction control the will, and it will equip the happy possessor for efficient service in the work of the church and in the reformation of society. Every associated effort in morals and religion will largely depend upon the faithfulness of the individuals who compose the band. The degree of efficiency can be gauged by the aggregated purpose of its members. That purpose becomes devout and resolute by communion with Christ, which is maintained in solitude. Herein lies the efficiency of associated efforts. Whatever tends to make it supreme, should be encouraged. Without it, the best plans, however well contrived, are doomed to failure.

This house is a monument of the devotion of its founders. But it will soon disappear. The insatiable encroachments of traffic have doomed it. In a few months you will be summoned to bid it farewell, and enter your new and beautiful sanctuary. It will be becoming to rehearse its history then. This monument shall be demolished, but its memorials shall survive, and grow richer and more lustrous as the ages roll. What reminiscences crowd upon our memories! If these walls were suddenly painted over as recollection with magical power retouches fading realities, what a gallery of portraits and processions would appear. The spectacle would bring back the fleeting years, and the faces and events most memorable. Here is the baptismal font where the seal of the sacred Trinity was set upon your brow. Here is the altar before which stood the affianced pair. Here seasons of communion left the impress of their sanctity upon some who went from this table to eat bread with the visible Christ in the upper sanctuary. Here with their dead have come the mourners clad in raiment of sorrow. With reverent hands we place their portraits on the walls, and commemorate their virtues.

If the pews could give a record of their occupants aroused to keen attention under the influences that have prevailed here, they would tell of souls convinced of the truth, softened into repentance, resolved to lead holier lives,—the tides of feeling swelling as the spirit of devotion was spread abroad in care-fraught minds, and the enfeebled purpose of duty made resolute, and the fascinations of the tempter grew dim in the beauty of grace, and the path of self-denial was no longer bitter but attractive when the print of the Saviour's feet was found thereon, and the thirst for gain was slaked by pouring upon it the sweet waters of charity, and the ties of brotherhood grew strong in the fellowship of Christ, and the feeble faith entered into peace at the exposure of unbelief, and the silent worship of the world's Creator was mingled with tears of gratitude in beholding Him here manifested in our nature to cleanse and redeem it, to comfort and enliven it, and exalt it to heaven.

A few of you in the Session and the choir, in the pew and the Sabbath school, who have trodden these courts since their origin, know their unwritten history for a longer period than the pastor, and recall scenes of surpassing interest which have been transacted here; but no one can weigh the tremendous import of the influences which have been poured like the waters of cleansing and refreshment upon the souls of the worshippers that have assembled here: when your prayers and benedictions, your songs of praise and the multitude of your thoughts have given inspiration to your minister, and by your looks of appreciation encouraged him to do his best in the pulpit and the study, in the prayer meeting and the parish, resorting to varied means and any change, to promote our common cause, and to make all men enter into the fellowship of the saints, and drink at the spring of their usefulness and joy.

Pray indulge me as the vision of these realities gathers upon the corridors of memory which we wander through to-day. Portraits that hung upon these walls are photographed upon my heart. Names seldom spoken now are voices in my ear; and many of the scenes half forgotten or dimly noticed then, are growing brighter as the mount grew radiant where Christ was transfigured and the voice was heard— "This is my beloved Son: hear Him." I see the multitude as they came and went; and some of them heard Him as ye have heard Him —yet not all.

My greatest grief is as I turn away, that some of you whom I love, and who have ever treated me with all the respect I deserve, do not

love the Master whose message I have faithfully delivered, and do not
treat Him with the confidence and devotion which his sacrifices for
you deserve. I have employed every mode of persuasion and illustration to convince you of the truth of the Gospel and its power to save
you. I have laid under tribute the realms of nature and revelation to
excite your trust in God who is the author of both. I have summoned
at the bar of your understanding the testimonies of men of every degree of knowledge, and of every age, differing in speech and education but agreeing in the approved and acceptable saying that "Jesus
Christ came into the the world to save sinners ;" and I have the testimony of my conscience that "I have not shunned to declare unto you
the whole counsel of God." O tempt the Lord no longer to say to his
messengers, "He is joined to his idols—let him alone!" You have lost
the ingenuousness of faith, and are wandering under the chill shadows
of skepticism. Let simple trust in Christ take possession of your heart,
and He will save you. O that this appeal to you might now be heeded !

I have no fears for any of you that are now the followers of the
crucified Son of God. For it is written :

1 John 2:1. "If any man sin we have an advocate with the Father,
even Jesus Christ the righteous."

We commit to Him our care. He covers us with the robe of His
righteousness here. We wear it into eternity. And lo ! He who sits
upon the throne is He that wrought it that they who wear it might be
transfigured into the image of Him who wove it upon the Cross for
them.

It may be expedient in the early history of a church to operate our
well-adjusted plan of government with allowance and concession ; for by
such adaptation the congregation, at first composed of heterogeneous
material, becomes united in spirit and harmonious in action—a constitu-
ency established upon principles held in common, and working out results
which its principles were designed to accomplish. A Presbyterian
church in doctrinal confession and Presbyterial connection has all the
elements of stability and progress. It is both radical and conservative,
regulated by law and yet free. Its temporal and spiritual affairs are
alike promoted by adherence to the principles that distinguish our

scriptural church which have won for it the admiration of observers in every land and age, and the enthusiastic love and devotion of its children.

I wish with all my heart to assist you and my successor to keep this church a God-fearing and Christ-honoring church that shall be known in heaven and on earth as an instrumentality wielded by the Holy Spirit to hasten the latter-day glory. May it ever have wisdom from above to choose pastors and elders and committees to carry out all plans for spiritual culture and church work; and then may its laity, who are the pillars of its stability and the artificers of its progress, be loyal to their leaders and faithful to their vows of support and co-operation.

To ask you to give my successsor a high place in your confidence were superfluous. Let him know that he possesses it by attempting no projects without his approval, and by supporting him in his plans to enlarge his usefulness, beginning at your own altars, and stretching forth your hands and voices to him.

Dear friends, though I leave you to represent the Synod of the Columbia in the training of the rising ministry, I shall retain my membership in the Presbytery to which this church belongs. To the members of the church and congregation I express my most grateful thanks for innumerable acts of kindness. I shall cherish in my inmost heart your forbearance, your sympathy, your appreciation and affection. You have held me up in my unresting labors by your generous support and your faithful prayers. I shall never forget how our souls have been lifted up on the wings of devotion and made better and more resolute by mutual help. These experiences no change of scene can blot out. God grant that the impressions made by the ministry that will soon close, may be purified from all imperfection by the Spirit of God, to guide and animate you in your pilgrimage, and remain upon the heart's imperishable tablets in eternity.

I can not speak the word that parts us.

GOOD MORNING! We shall meet again.

BENEDICTORY PRAYER AND DOXOLOGY.

For this cause I bow my knees unto the Father of our Lord Jesus Christ, of whom the whole family in heaven and earth is named, that he would grant you, according to the riches of his glory, to be strengthened with might by his Spirit in the inner man; that Christ may dwell in your hearts by faith; that ye, being rooted and grounded in love, may be able to comprehend with all saints what is the breadth, and length, and depth, and height; and to know the love of Christ, which passeth knowledge, that ye might be filled with all the fulness of God. Now unto him that is able to do exceeding abundantly above all that we ask or think, according to the power that worketh in us, unto him be glory in the church by Christ Jesus throughout all ages, world without end. Amen.

EPH. III:14-x

EXPLANATORY.—There are a few paragraphs and references in the foregoing pages which were not spoken when the discourse was delivered, in consequence of the pressure for time. They are now inserted according to the intention of the author to make the record more comprehensive. No attempt, however, has been made to compose a history.

Action of the Congregation.

At the close of the service a congregational meeting was held, at which a committee appointed to draft resolutions relative to the departure of Dr. Lindsley, presented the following report:

REPORT OF COMMITTEE ON RESOLUTIONS.

Mr. Chairman, Members of the Congregation:—At a meeting of the session of this church held on Monday evening, October 4th, our pastor, Rev. A. L. Lindsley, D. D., notified us of his intended resignation as pastor, and of his acceptance of the professorship in the Theological Seminary of San Francisco. The Session, after mature deliberation, consented to join in recommending the church to acquiesce in the dissolution of the pastoral relation by Presbytery.

On Thursday evening, October 7th, after the usual lecture, the congregation met and appointed a committee to draft a suitable expression of the sentiment of the congregation in view of the separation now about to take place.

On Sabbath morning, October 10th, 1886, the congregation assented to the recommendations of the Session and appointed three commissioners to attend Presbytery and make known the action of the Session and congregation.

Seldom does it devolve upon a committee to prepare resolutions touching a pastorate so rich in initial influences, so far-reaching in its importance and so well established in assured success. We have found it no easy matter to condense in a few lines the labors of eighteen years of faithful service. How far-reaching the influences which he has set in motion !

From Alaska to California the foundations have been laid. Missions have been established, churches organized, Sabbath schools planted and faithful teachers sent to nourish and to train. And now from these centers of influence, go streams which shall comfort and gladden the hearts of men till time shall end.

Divining from the first the breadth of the field, and the necessity for Christian activity in this rapidly growing country, with clear perception he has grasped the points of vantage, and planted the banner of the Master in many a waste place.

This people desire now to bear testimony to the pure consecration of life, the lofty aims, the loving personal ministry and faithfulness with which the gospel has been presented. During the more than nine hundred Sabbaths which he has served this people, the flock has not lacked food nor care.

The public, too, know where to find him, and their demands for his services have been numerous. Outside the regular Sabbath and week-day church services, he has been called to take part in protracted meetings, Y. M. C. A. services, public lectures, Sunday school conventions, Bible Society occasions, Seamen's Bethel, General Assembly, Synod, Presbytery, church dedications and temperance work. To have been ready on all these occasions with something to interest and instruct involves an amount of labor which is almost incalculable. A thorough consideration of these things will better enable us to appreciate his services.

It is largely due to him that Presbyterianism is so well established on this coast. Through him the Alaskans have the light of the Gospel, and competent ministers and teachers preach to and teach those who before were shut up to idolatry.

The Puyallup, the Umatilla and the Nez Perce Indians through him have competent ministers and teachers who declare unto them the Gospel. The Chinese, too, have not been forgotten or overlooked.

The twenty-two churches organized by him amongst our people, are sufficient proof that nothing in this line has been neglected.

But to this people he has faithfully declared the Word of God. He has ever held aloft the banner of Christ, and upon it has been that Name which is above every name. The whole trend of his public ministry has been to uphold believers, and bring sinners into the kingdom. He has been especially happy in comforting the sorrowing. There are not a few who in the presence of death, have heard words of comfort and peace, for which they will ever be grateful.

Sensible of the high honor conferred on Dr. Lindsley in his unanimous election to a chair in the Theological Seminary of the coast, we recognize with peculiar force his eminent fitness for that position. To it he will bring wide experience as a pastor, the culture of a scholar, and the wisdom and attractive power which have marked him as a leader in planning and furthering the manifold enterprises for the advancement of religion and education throughout the Northwest. In the higher field to which he is called, we shall pray that he may be eminently successful in training for the Master, men of pure, strong character, rich in faith and abounding in good works.

In parting with him we lose one whose name, wherever known, stands for that which is good and true. It is as a bulwark for the Church and religion throughout this coast.

At the beginning of his pastorate there were eighty-seven resident members. Since then seven hundred and forty have united. Four churches in the vicinity have been established by members from this church and more than $240,000 have been contributed by the congregation for various objects. The present membership is four hundred and twenty-three.

This church, nurtured and built up from small beginnings under his guidance and the blessing of God, to its present standing and influence, contemplates with deepest sorrow the severing of the ties that have united pastor and people, and desires now to unite in asking for him the blessings of that God whose word he has so faithfully declared, and the consolations of that grace he has so often administered to others.　　　　　　　　　　　　　　　　　H. W. CORBETT,
　　　　　　　　　　　　　　　　　　　　　　　　　G. M. WELLS,
　　　　　　　　　　　　　　　　　　　　　　　　　H. E. DOSCH,
　　　　　　　　　　　　　　　　　　　　　　　　　J. THORBURN ROSS,
　　　　　　　　　　　　　　　　　　　　　　　　　S. P. LEE.

After this report had been received and adopted by a unanimous rising vote, it was moved and carried in the same manner that Dr. Lindsley be requested to furnish the manuscript of his sermon for publication by the church.

Address by Rev. E. W. Garner, L.L.D.,

On Declaring the Pulpit Vacant Dec. 12, 1886.

You have now reached that period in your history when the pastoral connexion between you and my dear and honored brother, Dr. Lindsley, has come to an end ; and I feel that you cannot permit him to retire from the office he has so long retained without giving expression to the sincere and fervent desires of your hearts, and commending him to the special care of our Heavenly Father.

He has labored among you for the long period of eighteen years. Many of you think with gratitude to God, of the happy course of activity and usefulness which he has pursued. During that time there have been great changes in your midst, but you bless God that he sustained your beloved pastor by his grace, and enabled him to go forward in his work, carrying with him the affections of his people, and receiving many signs of the success of his labors.

You think with grateful pleasure of his *pulpit ministrations;* of the faithfulness with which you have been admonished ; and of the earnestness with which you have been warned. Many of you rejoice to think of him as the agent in your conversion ; and all of you devoutly bless God for those grand expositions of Divine truth which are exercising a moulding influence over your spiritual characters, and fitting you for the higher sphere of heavenly knowledge.

As a *pastor*, he never selfishly nor indolently shrank from the labor of serving you. In your homes you ever found him to be your friend. You have called him to the couch where your dear dying sufferers lay, and there in tenderness he has administered the consolations of the Gospel to both them and you. Therefore by your many family circles he will ever be greatly beloved. Your children have been taught to revere him; and there are many of you who have been trained from infancy under his instructions and who are thankful to be able to trace their effects in your hearts and lives.

The general conduct of Dr. Lindsley in public and private life, the uniformity of his fine Christian character, his high reputation, and his life, so singularly free from those blemishes which sometimes mar the character of public men, give cause for devout thankfulness. I need not refer to the academic honors, of your late pastor; honors deservedly bestowed and gracefully worn, nor to the many churches which he has been enabled to found in and around this city, as well as those in the East, nor to the obligations under which several institutions of learning are laid to him.

He was a great man everywhere, but was greatest in the pulpit. One who heard him so seldom as the present speaker is imperfectly qualified to form an accurate estimate of Dr. Lindsley's powers in this department, but I never could conceive it possible that an intelligent man could listen to him without deep impressions. He seized his subject strongly—with great originality—he developed it fully and effectively; scintillations of thought and power were struck from it at every wheel, and his affluence of illustration seemed to well out like an exhaustless stream.

There is a peculiar richness about his whole mental furniture, and there have been favorite themes on which he has kindled up with a divine fire, with something akin to the feelings of the seraphim, as they cry, "Holy, holy, holy," before the Lord of Hosts.

When I heard him in the pulpit I felt that he was a *man*, a holy man—it is true, yet a man, speaking unto men; and I candidly confess that but few ministers ever produced such an impression on my mind. There were two things which Dr. Lindsley, I believe, never did, and which he could not have done had he tried, viz., to make a *lean* sermon, or to deliver a sermon mechanically, without unction and fervor.

I have never heard him address an audience without doing ample justice to his subject, and without throwing himself heart and mind, with all their varied stores of rich thought and earnest feeling into the elucidation and enforcement of his theme. He was often carried away with the torrent of his conceptions and surcharged with an afflatus from the higher world. The impression produced by his handling of a subject, was not that it was exhausted, but that it was exhaustless. The more he talked, the more there seemed to be to say, and at the close, the untrodden field appeared much larger than the one actually surveyed. This was the feeling of all his thoughtful hearers : the more there was drawn out of him the more there was to come.

It was because of his many and varied excellencies that all eyes were turned to Dr. Lindsley, as the most suitable man to fill the new Theological chair, to which by the suffrage of his brethren he was called. May his last days be his best days.

And what shall I say to you, the members of this church and congregation? Whilst you are without a pastor stand firmly by one another, shoulder to shoulder. Give yourselves much to prayer for Divine direction. " Pray ye to the Lord of the harvest that *He* would send you a laborer" into your harvest field. Never did you stand in greater need of Divine guidance than now. Without *Him* you can do nothing but that which will make for your harm. I would recommend you to appoint a time for special prayer, that your Heavenly Father may give you a man after his own heart. All that I wish to say to you may be summed up in that one word—pray, and there need be no fear as to your future. " The Lord bless you and keep you. The Lord lift up His countenance upon you and give you peace."

By the authority vested in me by the Presbytery of Oregon, I hereby pronounce this pulpit vacant.